Small Wonders

poems by Norma Farber

woodcuts by Kazue Mizumura

COWARD, McCANN & GEOGHEGAN, INC.
NEW YORK

Some poems in this collection have appeared in the following sources:

Cricket magazine: "In the Park" (December 1975), "Turtle Song" (November 1976), "Spendthrift" (November 1976), "Forever Blowing" (March 1978), "The Rescue" (March 1978), "Taking Turns" (October 1978).

The Christian Science Monitor: "In Place of a Red Carpet" (July 8, 1964), "Going Round in a Square" (August 24, 1968, as "Walking the Curb"), "Finders Keepers" (May 21, 1976), "Praise to the Little" (September 30, 1976).

The Horn Book: "Sun for Breakfast" (April 1966).

Text copyright © 1964, 1968, 1975, 1976,
1978, 1979 by Norma Farber
Illustrations copyright © 1979 by Kazue Mizumura
All rights reserved. This book, or parts thereof,
may not be reproduced in any form without permission
in writing from the publishers. Published simultaneously
in Canada by Longman Canada Limited, Toronto.

Library of Congress Cataloging in Publication Data
Farber, Norma.
   Small wonders.
   SUMMARY: A collection of more than 20 poems about noise, the sun, flowers, and other topics.
   [1. American poetry.] I. Mizumura, Kazue.
II. Title.
PZ8.3.F224Sm   811'.5'4 78-31282 ISBN 0-698-20484-0

For Aileen Fisher

CONTENTS

Praise to the Little   6
In Place of a Red Carpet   7
Bandit Bee   8
Turtle Song   9
Sun After Rain   10
Taking Turns   11
I Hope She Won't Grow Any More   12
Night of the Half Moon   13
Sun for Breakfast   14
Carousel Brunch   15
In the Park   16
Spendthrift   17
Blow, Wind   18

Forever Blowing   19
The Washer-Waves   20
The Rescue   21
At the Ring of a Bell   22
For the Sewing Kit   22
Brown Eyes Are Watching   23
Bye Baby Walnut   24
Things As They Are   25
Going Round in a Square   26
Two of a Kind   27
In a Starry Orchard   28
Finders Keepers   29
The Noise of Nothing   30

PRAISE TO THE LITTLE

I lie in grass, I gaze content:
no need to stretch or stand,
while ants pay me the compliment
of climbing
                up
                        my
                                hand.

So tiny, trim, so trusting me:
how could I do them harm,
who demonstrate their confidence
by climbing
                down
                        my
                                arm?

IN PLACE OF A RED CARPET

If I had a ribbon, pure satin and red,
and wide as a snail in the grass—
before his small majesty lowly I'd spread
my cloth for his coming to pass.

I haven't a ribbon, of red or of satin—
not even the length of a string.
But he, from inside him, has rolled out a mat in
the path, where he goes like a king.

He royally moves on a silvery shine
of carpeting rarer than any of mine.

BANDIT BEE

A bee put on a zephyr,
and wore it as a boot,
then boldly made
a bee-line raid
on banks of honey-loot.

TURTLE SONG

Hard and slow,
I carry my house
wherever I go.

A creeping stone,
I carry my heavy
house of bone.

A turtle would ride—
if wishes were trailers—
soft inside.

Warm and well
and tender I'd travel—
without a shell.

SUN AFTER RAIN

Rain, rain,
went away.
Sun came out
with pipe of clay,
blew a bubble
whole-world-wide,
stuck a rainbow
on one side.

TAKING TURNS

When sun goes home
behind the trees,
and locks her shutters tight—

then stars come out
with silver keys
to open up the night.

I HOPE SHE WON'T GROW ANY MORE

Moon and her mother
came riding to town.
Moon said, O Mother,
please make me a gown!

Well, how shall I dress you—
as full, or as new,
my daughter—unless you
decide which is *you*?

And how shall I fit you,
in darkness, or glow?
Stand still as a statue:
I'll baste, I'll sew.

NIGHT OF THE HALF MOON

Half the moon's awake and gleaming.
The other's lying asleep, instead.
People would laugh
if only a half
of myself leaped up and out of bed—
and left the other half dreaming!

SUN FOR BREAKFAST

Rise up and look
at pond, at brook.

Night is now gone.
Morning upon
her silver tray
is serving day.

All you who wake
up hungry: take!

CAROUSEL BRUNCH

Merry-go-round
on the pepper mill!
My fingers ride
while fairgrounds spill
on bread, on butter,
on eggs, on tea.

My mother's
the cross calliope!

IN THE PARK

He who sits in the shade of his tail
has shelter in snow and rain and hail,
and a downy puff in December sleet,
and a parasol against August heat,
and a rudder to steer him, tree to tree,
and a parachute when he's falling free,
and a plume to wave to make himself known
to her who sits in a shade of her own.

SPENDTHRIFT

Coins—coins—coins—
a bushel to a breeze—
are pouring from the pockets
of the elm in the square.
Gather up the money-heaps—
as many as you please.
So rich an old tree
doesn't count them or care.

BLOW, WIND

I watched the waving milkweed tips,
   the soaring sail of thistle.

I thought I saw the wind's own lips
   purse up into a whistle.

FOREVER BLOWING

I lose the moments of my day
like foam that fizzles on the shore.
But fast as seconds hiss away,
the ocean pipes are blowing more.
I think that I shall never be
without some bubbles from the sea.

THE WASHER-WAVES

The waves come in on pearly toes.
The waves go out on blue.
They scrub the shore with tumbling snows.
They spread it out to bleach it new.
Their work, as everybody knows,
is never through.

Oh come and see the shining sands,
and praise the sea's hard-working hands.

THE RESCUE

When waves like tipping mirrors catch
fire from the glare of sun—
a foam-squad dashes over their backs
to dowse them, one by one.

AT THE RING OF A BELL

Sun is ringing a golden bell!
Rose, come crawling out of your shell!
Shy as a snail with quivering horns,
come out!   Be seen beyond the thorns!

FOR THE SEWING KIT

The dandelion's gone to seed,
the seed's swum off on fairy fins.
What's left's exactly what I need—
a white pin-cushion for my pins.

BROWN EYES ARE WATCHING

The deep brown eyes of susans
stretch open night and day.
But what they've spied,
so open-eyed,
they never, ever, say.

It should not be surprising
after the weeks they keep
watching away,
all night, all day—
they lean, they nod, they sleep.

BYE BABY WALNUT

Walnut in a walnut shell,
what a tiny wizened tot!
Cradle fits him very well—
till he wants a wider cot.

THINGS AS THEY ARE

Beetles that blow in the breeze
on stems—may be berries.

Marbles that grow on trees—
mostly are cherries.

GOING ROUND IN A SQUARE

Round and round—
in a square—
this curb I walk
won't go anywhere
except round and round
my neighborhood block,
round and round—
in a square!

Come join my circle,
you and you,
round and round
in a cornered queue,
round and round
our neighborhood block,
round and round—
in a square!

TWO OF A KIND

This manhole cover's just as neat
a decoration on our street
as that round moon upon its high
macadam avenue of sky.

IN A STARRY ORCHARD

Lean your ladder light
against a tree by night.

Climbing, examine how
stars hang on every bough.

Wearing a gossamer glove
on your right hand, remove

the ripest fruit of all:
that star about to fall.

FINDERS KEEPERS

Coming on the morning,
I shall find a day,
I shall find a golden find
before it fades away.

I shall find a twilight,
I shall find a sleep,
I shall find another day
to keep, keep, keep.

THE NOISE
OF NOTHING

The noise of nothing
is less than a pin
petering down
a deep apple bin,

less than a bubble,
blown round and ripe,
sliding up
off the brim of a pipe,

less than the ring
of a rain-drop gone
from the pool it tingled
and circled on,

less than a penny
put down in plush,
less than a web
where moth-wings hush,

less than a dew
the size of a drop,
drying by noon
on a petal's lip,

less than the hiss
if starlight fell
down the abyss
of a bottomless well,

less than something,
least of the small:
the noise of nothing's
no sound at all.

Has anyone heard it
breathe or blow?
ripple or stir?
No one I know.